TOYING
WITH TRIFLES

by

MARGARET HUTCHINGS

Lettering by Joseph J. Feesey
Line drawings by the author

MILLS & BOON LIMITED
50 Grafton Way, Fitzroy Square, London W.1

© *Margaret Hutchings 1960*
First published 1960
Second impression 1962
Third impression 1965
Fourth impression 1968

By the same author:
MODERN SOFT TOY-MAKING
DOLLS AND HOW TO MAKE THEM
THE BOOK OF THE TEDDY BEAR
HINTS ON SOFT TOYS
PATCHWORK PLAYTHINGS

for children
WHAT SHALL I DO WITH THIS?
WHAT SHALL I DO THIS MONTH?
WHAT SHALL I DO TODAY?
WHAT SHALL I DO FROM SCANDINAVIA?

To all my small friends who sucked so hard (and so willingly) to provide the lolly sticks—with love from "Mrs Margaret"

SBN 263 70034 8

*Made and printed in Great Britain
by Jarrold & Sons Ltd, Norwich*

CONTENTS

iii

How the Trifles became Toys

Have you ever sat waiting for something, a telephone call perhaps or the start of a new lesson, and suddenly found you had unconsciously been "doodling"? You may join up lines, shade in shapes, draw a series of circles and often an amusing little figure emerges.

These toys began in just that way (only in "3D"), when having been asked for ideas for very simply made toys, I sat thinking, and absent-mindedly fiddling with a pile of trifles on my work-bench. These were the sort of trifles every household contains and which no toy-maker discards—just in case! Quite suddenly, strange little men and animals began to take shape. The date-box became a dog's body, the lolly sticks legs for all kinds of beasties, the cotton-reels a caterpillar, and within a few hours quite a procession had materialised.

These are not toys in the true sense of the word, and are certainly not exhibition pieces! They are, however, the greatest fun to make, as well as being easy and very cheap. Everyone who can use a needle can make them, as only simple oversewing is needed; therefore mothers and daughters of all ages, grannies and even younger sons can combine in one co-operative effort.

When some of you met Percy the Pill-box-head Penguin and his relations on television, you asked for a book of ideas on turning your trifles into toys. Here it is, and I hope you will have lots of fun trying out first these ideas, then toying with any other trifles you can manage to collect.

M. H.

Things to remember before you start toying

1. Use clean tins, never rusty ones.
2. If these are the type with a depression at the top (scouring powder) or in the lid (golden syrup), fill up the hollow with wadding before covering.
3. Never use glass or breakable containers.
4. Fill soft containers (cigarette boxes) with fine shavings or something light before covering, to avoid crushing.
5. Pill boxes may be bought for a penny or two from any chemist. If they are too deep (e.g. for Penguin's hat) cut them down.
6. Eyes may be either sewn on before or stuck on after covering containers.
7. Use Copydex for all sticking jobs.
8. Measurements given are only a rough guide—as are the colour suggestions. Plan your toys to suit whatever trifles you happen to have.
9. All patterns may be traced from the book and are of a suitable size for a toy made to the measurements given in each case, but they can easily be varied.
10. All rolls of felt (fig. 3) should be about $\frac{1}{2}$ inch across, unless for a large, heavy toy, when they should be about $\frac{3}{4}$ inch.
11. For very awkward jobs, try a curved surgical needle, bought from a chemist.
12. If fur is unobtainable find a substitute—fringed felt perhaps.
13. Although felt is generally recommended, scraps of other material may be used instead. This is not so easy to deal with because of the raw edges, but will present no problems to the average needlewoman.
14. Sew with Sylko.

3

How to put the Toys together

Fig. 1

COVERING TINS, BOXES AND REELS
WITH FELT

A. Cut a strip of felt to fit round the edge. Oversew in place.
B. Cut two shapes to fit top and bottom of the container, by placing it on the felt and drawing all round; oversew these in place.

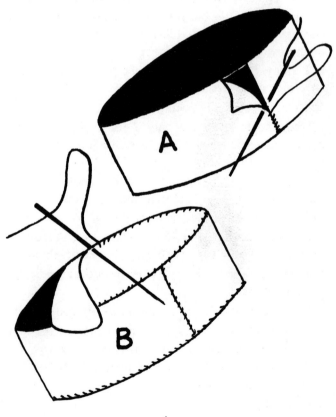

Fig. 2

JOINING TWO CONTAINERS TOGETHER
(*A*, head to body; *B*, legs to body)

Use a long, slim needle and strong cotton or double Sylko; work in ladder stitch (one stitch alternately on each container). Pull stitches tight to draw the two together. Stitch on both sides. Work in just the same way when joining legs to a body (e.g. Baby Bear, when you join reels to a tin, or Gollywog's legs, which are rolls of felt); these are circular and are ladder-stitched all round.

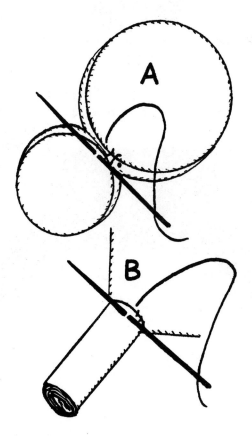

Goofy the Golly

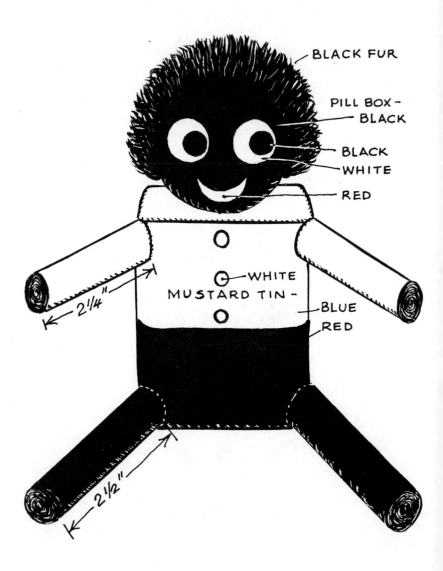

BLACK FUR

PILL BOX —
BLACK

BLACK
WHITE

RED

WHITE
MUSTARD TIN —

BLUE
RED

2¼"

2½"

YOU WILL NEED:

One 4-oz. rectangular mustard tin for the body.
One 1½-inch pill-box for the head.
One narrow strip of black fur for hair (3 inches).
Scraps of red, blue, black, and white felt.

HOW TO MAKE HIM:

Cover the tin, top half blue, lower half red. Cover the pill-box with black felt (fig. 1). Sew head to body. Make two rolls of red felt (fig. 3) 2½ inches long for legs and two of blue 2¼ inches long for arms.

Sew these in place at the front four corners of the tin. Sew on hair. Cut out eyes, pupils, mouth and buttons, tracing the patterns from the picture, and stick in place.

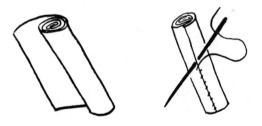

Fig. 3. Making rolls of felt for limbs.

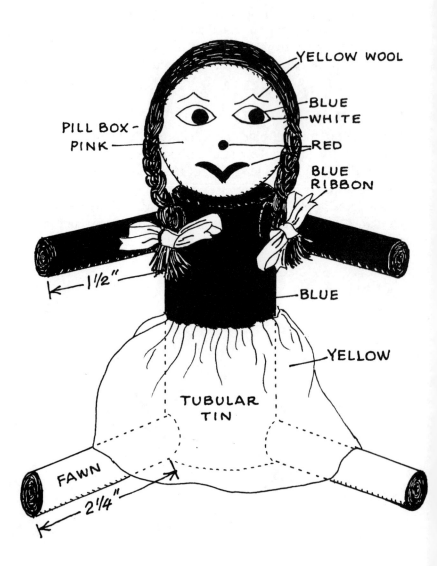

YELLOW WOOL

BLUE
WHITE

PILL BOX-
PINK

RED

BLUE
RIBBON

1½"

BLUE

YELLOW

TUBULAR
TIN

FAWN

2¼"

8

Tube-tin Topsy

YOU WILL NEED:

One tubular tin $2\frac{3}{4}$ inches high for body.
One $1\frac{1}{2}$-inch pill-box for the head.
A few yards of yellow wool for hair.
$\frac{1}{2}$ yard very narrow blue ribbon for bows.
Scraps of red, blue, yellow, white, pink, fawn felt.

HOW TO MAKE HER:

Cover the tin with blue and the box with pink felt (fig. 1). Sew head to body (fig. 2). Make two rolls of blue felt $1\frac{1}{2}$ inches long for arms and two of fawn $2\frac{1}{4}$ inches long for legs (fig. 3). Sew these in place, copying picture. Cut a strip of yellow felt $1\frac{3}{4}$ inches wide and 8 inches long. Join the two short ends. Run a gathering thread all round one edge, place on doll for a skirt, pull up gathers to fit and stitch in place. Cut mouth and nose in red, outer eyes in white and inner eyes in blue felt, tracing patterns from the picture, and stick in place. Cut 36 strands of yellow wool (3-ply) $5\frac{1}{2}$ inches long. Squeeze some Copydex on to top of head, place the wool on this, press firmly and stick in position for hair. Make a plait each side and tie a small bow on the end of each. Embroider eyebrows with yellow wool.

Topsy could have buttons on her jersey and an embroidered skirt. She could wear a hat like the penguin on page 50, or have short curly hair, made by stitching "loops" of yellow wool all over the top of her head.

Mustard-tin Mickey
Match-box Mandarin

LOOPS OF YELLOW WOOL

3/4 CIRCLE OF BLACK FELT

1½" PILL BOX

1½" PILL BOX

2 OZ. MUSTARD TIN

BLACK PLAITED WOOL

←1¼"→

←1½"→

MATCH BOX

3¾"

When you have made Goofy and Topsy, try inventing some more dolls from different shaped tins and boxes. Here are some pictures to help you. You could make several little men* and sit them on a wall made from a tin or box covered with red felt. Embroider the bricks first, using thick, white stranded cotton and stem stitch.

* For ideas for other little tin men see *Modern Soft Toy Making*, Section IV.

10

Pill-box Piccaninny

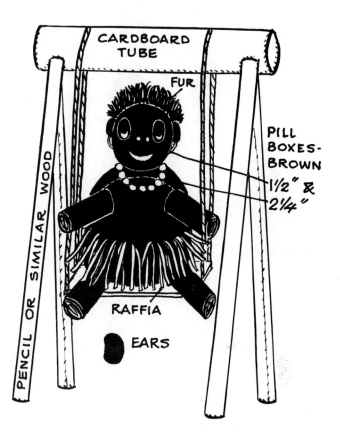

The piccaninny's skirt is short pieces of raffia sewn all round her waist; she has fur hair and two tiny rings sewn to her ears. Try making a swing and sew one of the dolls to the seat. Pencils or odd pieces of cane make good posts, a cardboard tube the top, and a piece of thick card, the seat. Cover them all with fawn felt and use string for "ropes".

Now think up some more ideas. Nursery rhyme characters would be fun—you could start with Jack Horner or Boy Blue.

11

Baby Bear

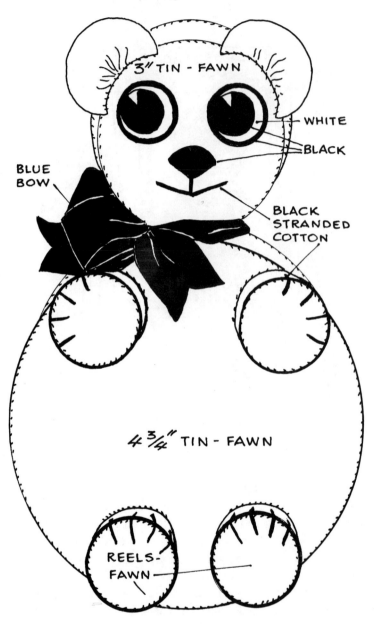

3" TIN - FAWN

WHITE

BLACK

BLUE BOW

BLACK STRANDED COTTON

4 3/4" TIN - FAWN

REELS- FAWN

YOU WILL NEED:

Two round, flat tins (4¾ and 3 inches) for head and body.
Four Sylko reels for arms and legs.
Fawn felt and scraps of black and white.
Black stranded cotton.
½ yard of blue ribbon for the neck.

HOW TO MAKE HIM:

Cover the tins and reels with fawn felt (fig. 1). Join head to body (fig. 2), and sew arms and legs in position, copying picture.

Using the pattern at the foot of this page, cut out and sew on ears. Cut out eyes and nose, tracing the patterns from the picture, and stick in place. Using an extra long, fine, darning needle, embroider mouth and "claws" with long straight stitches. Tie a bow of ribbon round the bear's neck.

On the next page is a cat made in just the same way, but with his head on one side. Try making the bear like this for a change.

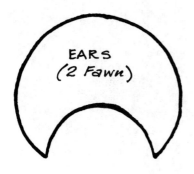

EARS
(2 Fawn)

13

Columbus the Cat

YOU WILL NEED:

Two round, flat tins (4¾ and 3 inches) for head and body.
Two shallow pill-boxes (1¼ inches) for feet.
Black felt and scraps of white and green.
Stiff white thread for whiskers.
White stranded cotton.
½ yard pink ribbon for the neck.

HOW TO MAKE HIM:

Cover the tins and boxes with black felt (fig. 1). Join head to body (fig. 2), and sew feet in place, copying picture. Be careful to balance the head and feet so that the cat sits firmly. Using the pattern at the foot of this page, cut out ears and sew to head. Trace eyes, nose and mouth from pictures and stick in place. Make whiskers from lengths of thick, white thread or horsehair threaded into place with a long needle. Embroider "claws" in white stranded cotton, using a long fine darning needle and straight stitches. Make a slim roll of black felt 5 inches long (fig. 3) and stitch to back of cat for a tail. Tie a bow of pink ribbon round his neck.

Try making a family of cats and kittens, using different coloured felt. Round cheese-boxes will do instead of tins. Some of them could have their heads straight like the bear, some bending to the left and some to the right.

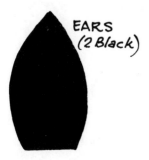

EARS
(2 Black)

15

More Roly-Poly Rascals

ROBERT THE RABBIT

POPPET THE PANDA

OSWALD THE OWL

EGBERT THE ELEPHANT

When you have made the bear and cat on pages 12 and 14 you might like to try out more ideas for sitting animals and birds, made from two flat round tins. These pictures will help you to start, and you will be able to think out many more of your own.

The cat would easily turn into a lion if you made him in fawn and stitched a piece of fur round his head for a mane. He would make a sitting companion to the Lovable Lion on page 30. You could make the Three Bears, using various-sized tins and turning Tube-tin Topsy (page 8) or Simpering Cynthia (page 26) into Goldilocks.

For the rabbit's ears use the pattern on page 19. A pattern for the elephant's ear is given below.

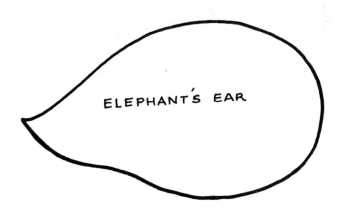

ELEPHANT'S EAR

Little Brown Rabbit

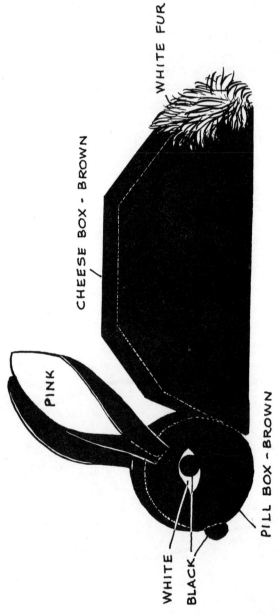

WHITE FUR

CHEESE BOX - BROWN

PINK

PILL BOX - BROWN

WHITE

BLACK

YOU WILL NEED:

   1 cheese-box (semicircular or as picture) for body.
   1 pill-box (1¾ inches) for head.
   A tiny piece of white fur for tail.
   Brown felt and scraps of black, white and pink.

HOW TO MAKE HIM:

Cover the boxes with brown felt (fig. 1) and join head to body (fig. 2). Sew the fur in place for tail. Cut out the ears, eyes, pupils and nose, using patterns at the foot of this page. Stick eyes in position. Run a gathering thread all round outside edge of nose, pull up and stuff with a tiny piece of cotton wool so as to form a round "knob". Sew to head. Stick the pink ear-linings to the brown ears, fold as shown in picture and stitch this fold securely in place. Sew ears to head.

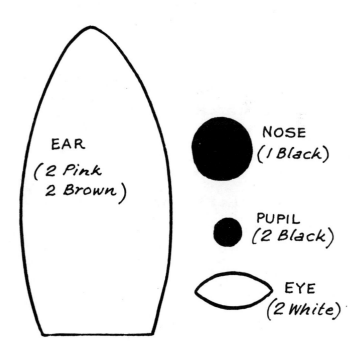

EAR
(2 Pink
   2 Brown)

NOSE
(1 Black)

PUPIL
(2 Black)

EYE
(2 White)

Lolly Stick Swan

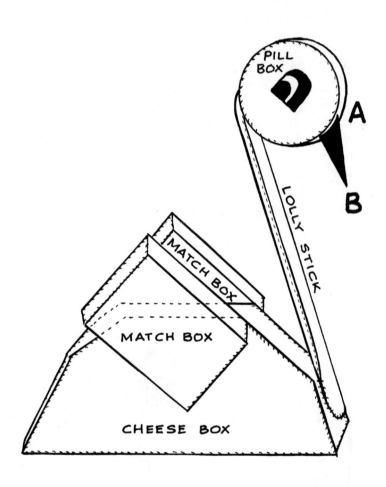

YOU WILL NEED:

1 cheese-box (semicircular or as picture) for body.
1 pill-box (1¾ inches) for head.
2 match-boxes for wings.
1 lolly stick for neck.
White felt and scraps of black and orange.

HOW TO MAKE HIM:

Cover the boxes (fig. 1) and lolly stick (fig. 4) with white felt.

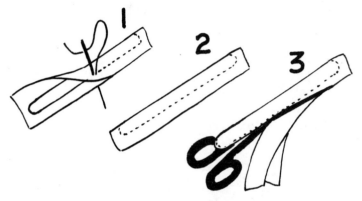

Fig. 4. Covering a lolly stick.

Sew together, copying picture. Cut out eyes, pupils and beak, using patterns at the foot of this page. Stick eyes in place. Fold beak in half so that *A*'s meet and oversew *A–B*. Stitch in place on head.

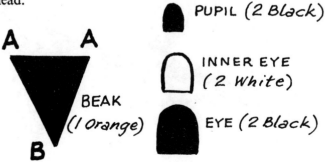

PUPIL (*2 Black*)

A   A

INNER EYE
(*2 White*)

BEAK
(*1 Orange*)

EYE (*2 Black*)

B

21

Two Ducks on a See-Saw

When you have made the rabbit and swan on pages 18 and 20, try making a collection of ducks. Here are two ideas for you to start with. If you have an old ruler or similar shaped piece

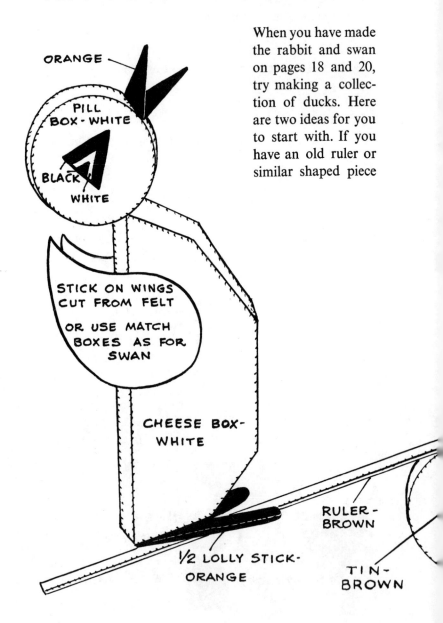

ORANGE

PILL BOX - WHITE

BLACK

WHITE

STICK ON WINGS CUT FROM FELT

OR USE MATCH BOXES AS FOR SWAN

CHEESE BOX - WHITE

RULER - BROWN

½ LOLLY STICK - ORANGE

TIN - BROWN

of wood you could cover it with brown felt for a see-saw. Make the "log" from a tin and sew the "plank" firmly in place and the ducks to the plank.

Now turn the standing duck into a penguin, copying the colour and markings from the one on page 50.

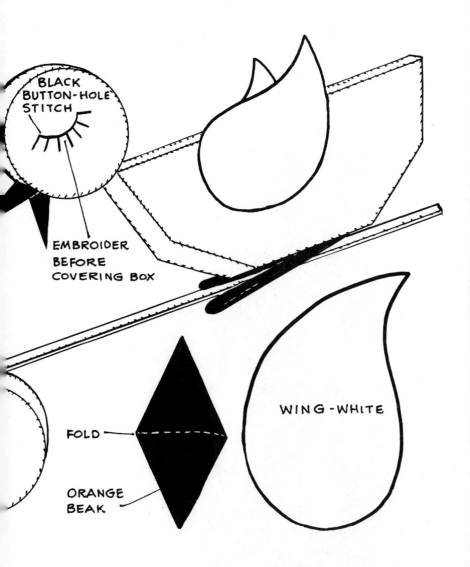

BLACK
BUTTON-HOLE
STITCH

EMBROIDER
BEFORE
COVERING BOX

WING-WHITE

FOLD

ORANGE
BEAK

Salty Sam

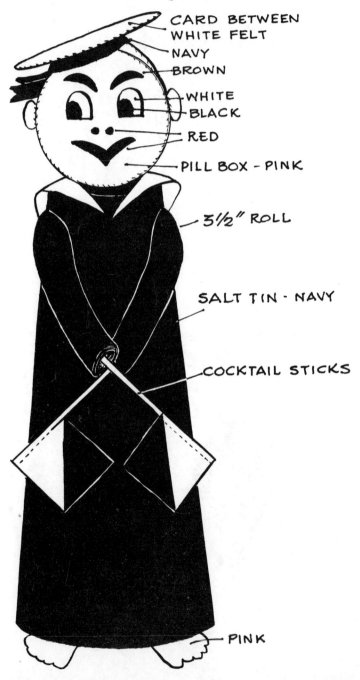

YOU WILL NEED:

One Sifta salt tin for the body.
One pill-box (2½ inches) for the head.
One circle of card (2¾ inches diameter) for hat.
Two cocktail sticks.
Navy-blue felt and scraps of pink, white, red and brown.

HOW TO MAKE HIM:

Cover the tin with navy and the box with pink felt (fig. 1). Sew head to body (fig. 2). Make two rolls of navy felt 3½ inches long for arms (fig. 3). Sew in place. Cut out pieces given at the foot of this page. Stick on features and feet. Sew on ears and collar. Place the card between two slightly larger circles of felt, oversew all round edge. Sew to head for hat. Stick a strip of felt 8 inches by ½ inch all round head, allowing two tails to hang down back for ribbons. Make two semaphore flags, 1¼ inches square, with cocktail stick handles, push into ends of arms and stitch in place.

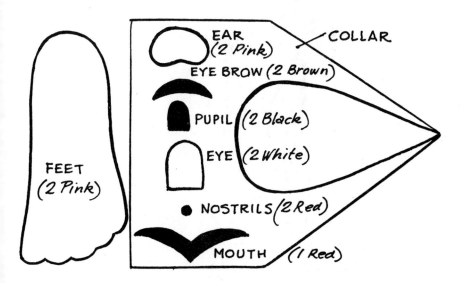

FEET
(2 Pink)

EAR
(2 Pink)

COLLAR

EYE BROW (2 Brown)

PUPIL (2 Black)

EYE (2 White)

NOSTRILS (2 Red)

MOUTH (1 Red)

Simpering Cynthia

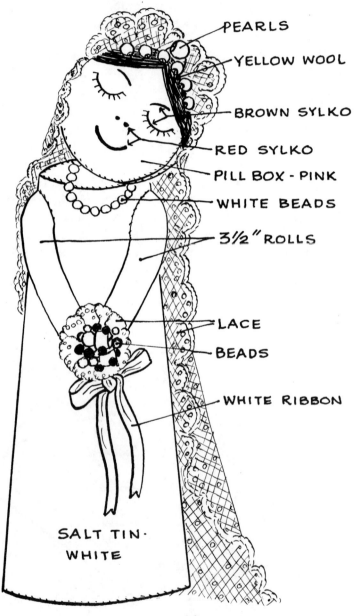

PEARLS

YELLOW WOOL

BROWN SYLKO

RED SYLKO

PILL BOX - PINK

WHITE BEADS

3½" ROLLS

LACE

BEADS

WHITE RIBBON

SALT TIN·
WHITE

YOU WILL NEED:

One Sifta salt tin for the body.
One pill-box (2½ inches) for the head.
White felt and a scrap of pink.
Yellow wool for hair.
About ¾ yard lace 3 inches wide for veil.
About 4 inches lace ¾ inch wide for bouquet.
¼ yard white ribbon ½ inch wide for bouquet.
Pearls and pink, blue, green and white beads.
Brown and red Sylko for features.

HOW TO MAKE HER:

Cut the pink felt pieces for covering box and embroider features
with Sylko on one of the circles. Cover box (fig. 1). Cover tin
with white felt (fig. 1). Sew head to body, giving it a forwards
and sideways tilt as picture. Embroider hair with yellow wool,
using long, straight stitches. Make two rolls of white felt
3½ inches long for arms (fig. 3), and sew in place. Gather the
narrow lace along one edge, pull up to form a circle, sew to
arms as picture. Sew on coloured beads for flowers. Tie the
ribbon in a small bow with long ends and sew to base of
bouquet. Make a small necklace of white beads and stitch in
place on shoulders. Fold the wide lace in half lengthwise and
stitch the centre part to top of head for a veil, gathering it into
place. Join the two straight edges of the lace all down centre
back, so that the veil forms a train. Sew on pearls for head-dress.

If you have no lace you could make a net veil, and this could
cover the face. If you have no beads try making felt flowers as
for the bridesmaid on page 28.

Cynthia's Wedding Group

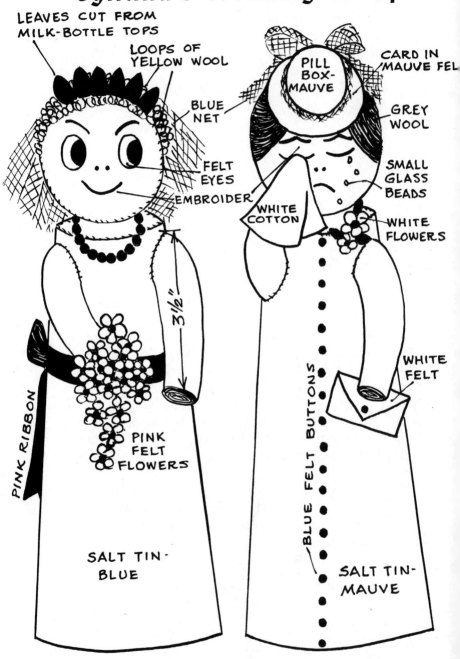

LEAVES CUT FROM MILK-BOTTLE TOPS

LOOPS OF YELLOW WOOL

BLUE NET

FELT EYES

EMBROIDER

PINK RIBBON

PINK FELT FLOWERS

SALT TIN-BLUE

3½"

CARD IN MAUVE FEL

PILL BOX-MAUVE

GREY WOOL

SMALL GLASS BEADS

WHITE COTTON

WHITE FLOWERS

WHITE FELT

BLUE FELT BUTTONS

SALT TIN-MAUVE

CHIEF BRIDESMAID

BRIDE'S MOTHER

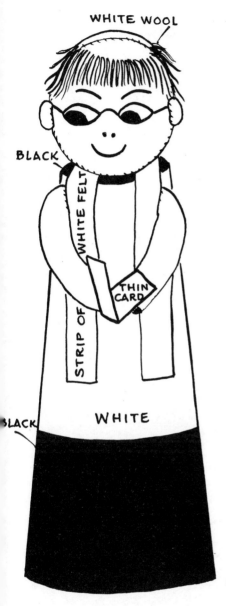

WHITE WOOL

BLACK

WHITE FELT

THIN CARD

STRIP OF

BLACK

WHITE

THE PARSON

When you have made Cynthia, perhaps you would like to build other figures and make a whole wedding group. You could use the bridegroom on page 38 or give her a naval or military wedding with Salty Sam or Tubular Tommy. Here are three ideas for people at the wedding; then think out some of your own. Don't forget the best man, choir boys, bridegroom's parents, photographer and all the wedding guests. Try turning Topsy and Mickey (pages 8 and 10) into train-bearers, and use a salt tin upside down for some of the men, in the same way as the policeman on page 2; this gives a broad-shouldered effect. Perhaps you could make a wedding cake from various-sized pill-boxes covered with white felt, and cocktail stick pillars.

PETALS   CENTRES   LEAVES

PATTERNS FOR FLOWERS

A Lovable Lion

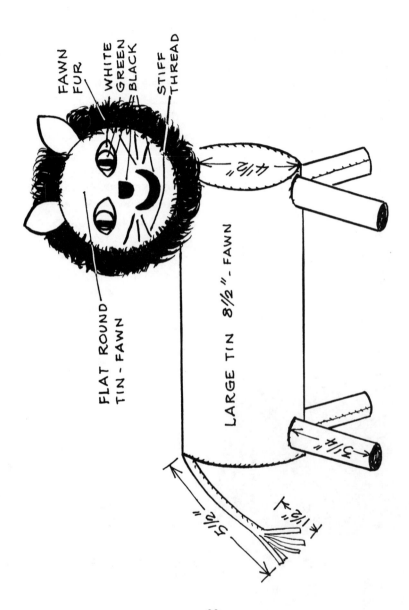

FAWN FUR

WHITE
GREEN
BLACK

STIFF THREAD

4½"

FLAT ROUND TIN – FAWN

LARGE TIN 8½" – FAWN

3¼"

5½"

1½"

YOU WILL NEED:

One flat, round tin (4¾ inches) for head.
One large tin (8½ inches long) for body.
Fawn felt and scraps of green, white and black.
A narrow strip of fawn fur for mane.
Stiff white thread for whiskers.

HOW TO MAKE HIM:

Cover tins with fawn felt (fig. 1). Sew head to body (fig. 2). Cut out and sew on ears. Make four fat rolls of fawn felt 3¼ inches long for legs (fig. 3). Sew to body. Make a slim roll of fawn felt 5½ inches long for tail. Seam the first 4 inches and fringe the end 1½ inches. Sew in place. Cut out and stick in place eyes, pupils, iris, nose and mouth. Sew on mane. With an extra long, slim needle stitch short lengths of stiff white thread through the front of the face for whiskers.

If the legs are not sufficiently steady for the weight of your tins, use covered Smartie tubes (cut down to 3½ inches) instead.

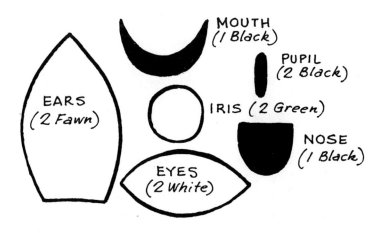

EARS
(2 Fawn)

MOUTH
(1 Black)

PUPIL
(2 Black)

IRIS (2 Green)

NOSE
(1 Black)

EYES
(2 White)

A Plump Pink Pig

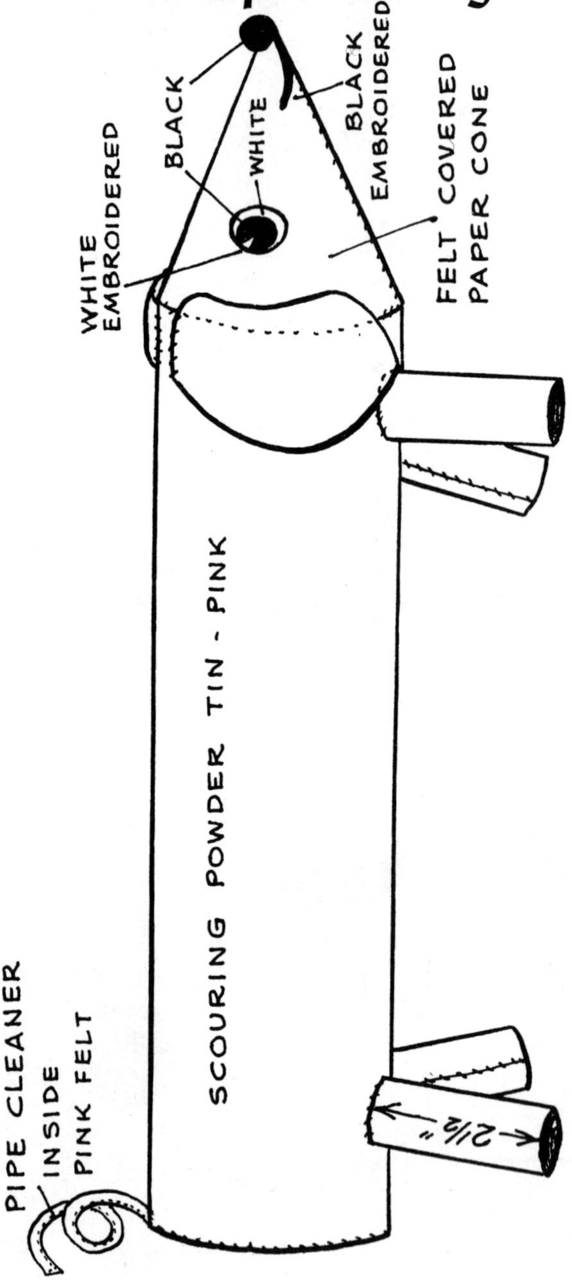

BLACK

WHITE

BLACK EMBROIDERED

WHITE EMBROIDERED

FELT COVERED PAPER CONE

SCOURING POWDER TIN - PINK

PIPE CLEANER INSIDE PINK FELT

2½"

YOU WILL NEED:

One scouring powder tin for body.
One pipe-cleaner for tail.
A piece of stiff paper for head ($7 \times 3\frac{1}{2}$ inches).
Pink felt and scraps of black and white.
Black and white stranded cotton.

HOW TO MAKE HIM:

Cover the tin with pink felt (fig. 1). Cover the pipe-cleaner to
match, working as for the lolly stick (fig. 4). Make four fat rolls
of pink felt $2\frac{1}{2}$ inches long (fig. 3) for the legs. Cut a semicircle
of paper and one of pink felt as shown below, for head. Stick
felt to paper. Twist into cone to fit end of tin and stitch. Cut
out ears, eyes, pupils and nose. Sew head, tail, legs and ears to
body. Curl tail. Stick on eyes. Run a gathering thread all round
outside edge of nose, pull up to form a round knob, put a tiny
piece of stuffing inside, sew to head. Embroider mouth and
highlight on eyes.

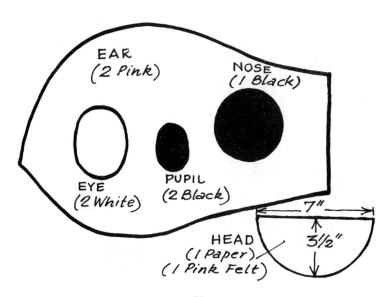

EAR
(2 Pink)

NOSE
(1 Black)

EYE
(2 White)

PUPIL
(2 Black)

HEAD
(1 Paper)
(1 Pink Felt)

7"

3½"

A Handsome Horse

When you have made the lion and pig, try making this horse. He is grey, with black hoofs, fur mane and tail and pink saddle and reins. The cardboard tubes came from rolls of kitchen paper and were cut to the correct length.

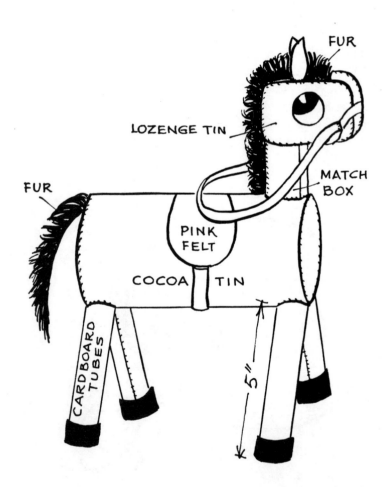

A Dizzy Dog

This dog is white with black spots and a red collar. He is not quite so easy to make as some of the other toys.

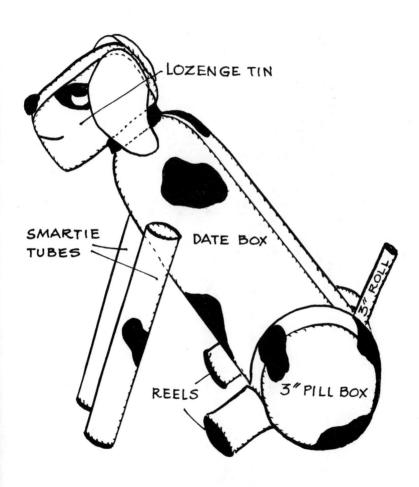

LOZENGE TIN

SMARTIE TUBES

DATE BOX

3" ROLL

REELS

3" PILL BOX

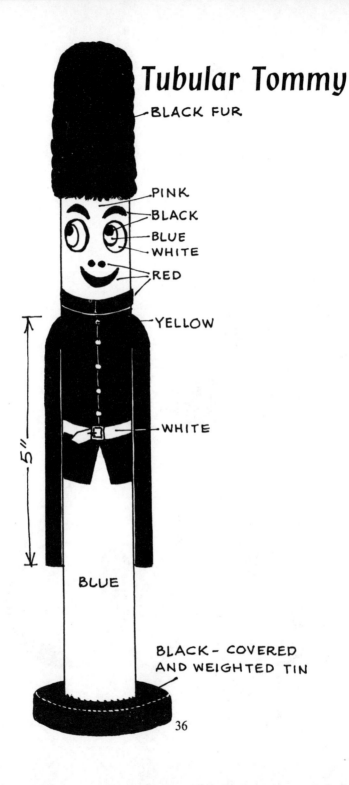

Tubular Tommy

BLACK FUR

PINK
BLACK
BLUE
WHITE
RED

YELLOW

WHITE

5"

BLUE

BLACK – COVERED
AND WEIGHTED TIN

36

YOU WILL NEED:

One tubular container (Flower Lights) or cardboard roll
(15½ inches tall) for body.
One small round tin (2¾ inches) for base.
Heavy nails, stones or the like for weights.
Small piece of black fur for busby.
Red, blue, black, white, pink and yellow felt.
Black stranded cotton.

HOW TO MAKE HIM:

Fill the tin with something heavy, so as to give weight at the
base; cover this with black felt (fig. 1).

Cut a piece of blue felt 7 inches long to fit round the tube,
and stick firmly in place for trousers; seam at centre back. Cut
a piece of pink felt 3 inches long and stick in place for face;
seam at centre back. Cut a piece of red felt 4 inches long and
stick in place for jacket; seam at centre front (overlap trousers
and face). Seam only the top 2½ inches, leaving the lower 1½
inches loose and open at front as picture. Cut out the features
as given; stick in place. Cut and stick on a strip of red felt for
collar, and white felt for belt, having the belt about ½ inch too
long so that it overlaps in front as picture. Cut the end to a
point, embroider a buckle in black stranded cotton. Make two
rolls of red felt 5 inches long (fig. 3), and stitch in place for
arms, catching firmly to sides. Cut a piece of black fur 4 inches
long for busby—seam across top and down centre back on the
wrong side, reverse, ease on to head and stitch in place. Lastly,
sew Tommy to the prepared base.

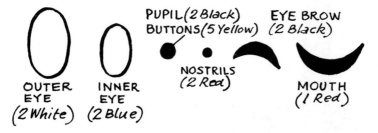

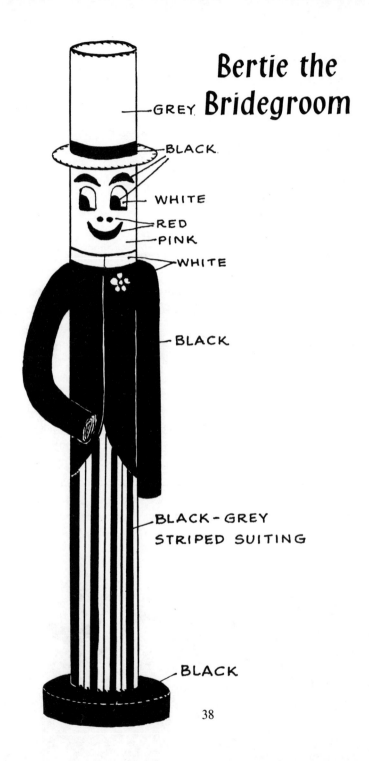

Bertie the **Bridegroom**

GREY

BLACK

WHITE

RED

PINK

WHITE

BLACK

BLACK-GREY
STRIPED SUITING

BLACK

38

YOU WILL NEED:

One tubular container (Flower Lights) or cardboard roll
   (15½ inches tall) for body.
One small round tin (2¾ inches) for base.
Heavy nails, stones or the like for weights.
Circle of cardboard (2½ inches) for hat brim.
Small piece of black/grey striped suiting for trousers.
Black, white, pink, red, grey and yellow felt.

HOW TO MAKE HIM:

Prepare base as for Tubular Tommy. Cut a piece of suiting
7 inches long, stick in place for trousers, turning the raw edge
under at the bottom and the two raw edges inwards at centre
back seam. Cut a strip of pink felt 3 inches long, stick in place
for face, seam at centre back. Cut a piece of black felt 5½ inches
long, stick in place for coat, seam at centre front. Stick only the
top 4 inches, leaving the lower 1½ inches open; cut away each
side as picture. Make two rolls of black felt 5 inches long
(fig. 3) and stitch in place for arms, one straight and one bent.
Cut eyes and pupils as given at the foot of this page and eyebrows, nostrils and mouth as given on page 37; stick in place.
Cut a piece of grey felt 3 inches long for hat, stick in place, seam
at centre back. Place top of tube on centre of cardboard circle,
draw all round. Cut away inner circle and cover cardboard ring
with grey felt, oversewing all round inner and outer circle. Ease
on to tube, stitch in place for hat brim. Cut a strip of black felt
for hat band and white felt for collar, stick in place. Make a
white flower as on page 29 for buttonhole. Sew bridegroom to
the base.

EYE
(2 White)

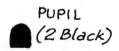
PUPIL
(2 Black)

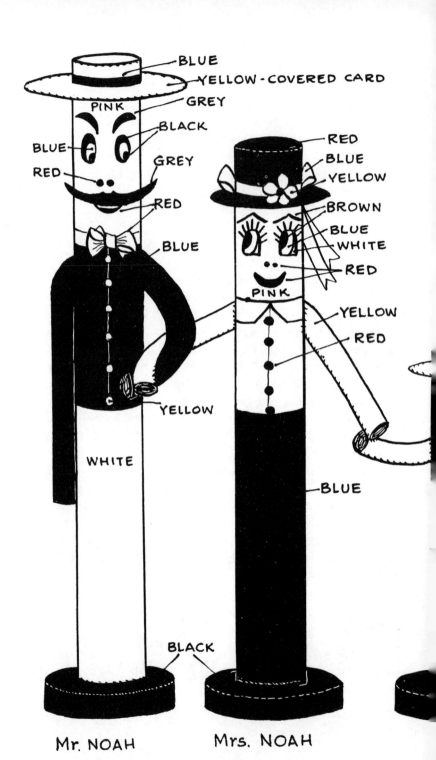

Mr. NOAH   Mrs. NOAH

The Noah Family

If you can collect cardboard rolls or tubular containers of different lengths and thickness, you could make whole families of these dolls. Here is an idea for making Mr and Mrs Noah and their children. Once you have made Tommy and the Bridegroom you will not find these difficult and will be able to invent many more characters yourself.

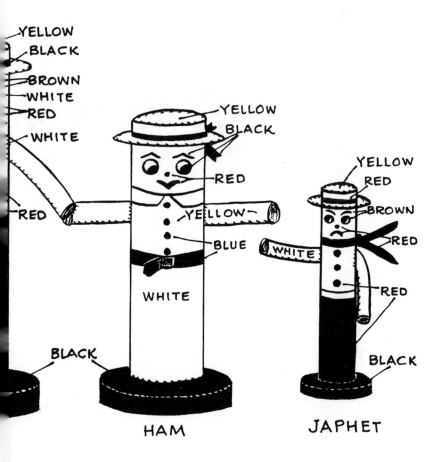

HAM

JAPHET

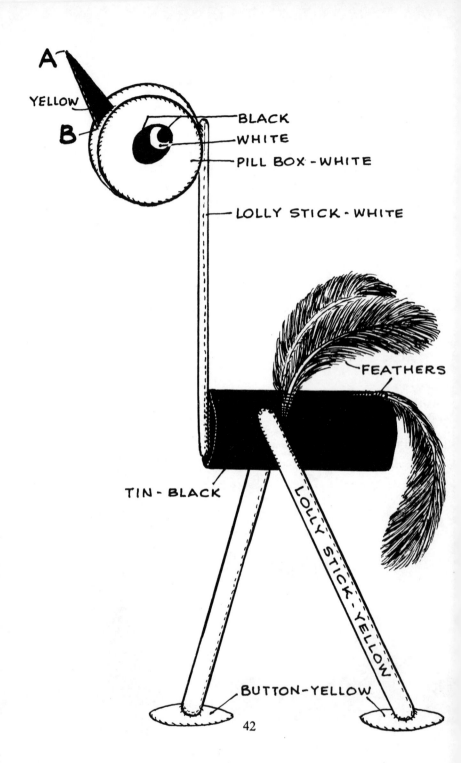

A

YELLOW

B

BLACK

WHITE

PILL BOX - WHITE

LOLLY STICK - WHITE

FEATHERS

TIN - BLACK

LOLLY STICK - YELLOW

BUTTON - YELLOW

Olive the Offended Ostrich

YOU WILL NEED:

One tubular tin for body.
One pill-box (1½ inches) for head.
Three lolly sticks for legs and neck.
Two buttons (1¼ inches) for feet.
Three small chicken feathers for wings and tail.
Scraps of black, white and yellow felt.

HOW TO MAKE HER:

Cover the tin with black, the box (fig. 1), and one lolly stick
(fig. 4) with white, the other two lolly sticks and the buttons
with yellow felt. Cut out the pieces as given at the foot of this
page. Fold beak in half so that the B's meet and oversew seam
A–B. Copying picture, sew to head. Stick eyes in place. Sew
head to neck, and neck to body. Sew covered buttons in place
on the end of the yellow-covered lolly sticks for feet. Do this
very securely so that the finished toy does not wobble. Sew tops
of legs to body. Sew the feathers in place.

Try making a family of these birds, giving each one a different
expression by varying the position of eyes and beaks. You could
easily turn her into a flamingo or stork with a little imagination.

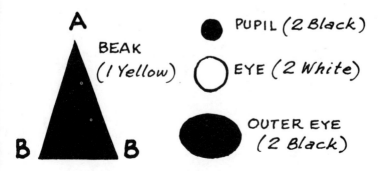

A

BEAK
(1 Yellow)

B   B

PUPIL (2 Black)

EYE (2 White)

OUTER EYE
(2 Black)

43

George the Gigantic Giraffe

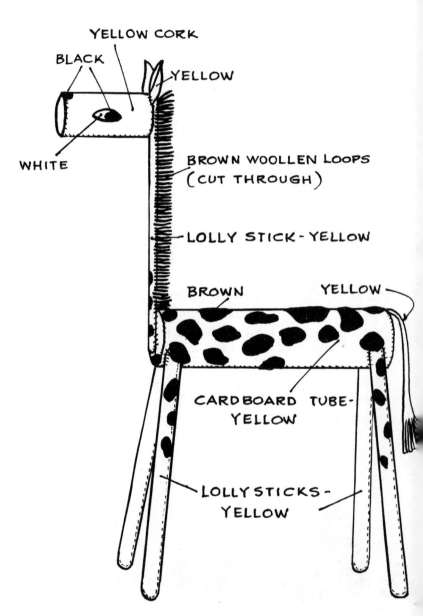

YELLOW CORK

BLACK

YELLOW

WHITE

BROWN WOOLLEN LOOPS
(CUT THROUGH)

LOLLY STICK - YELLOW

BROWN

YELLOW

CARDBOARD TUBE-
YELLOW

LOLLY STICKS-
YELLOW

YOU WILL NEED:

One cardboard tube ($3\frac{1}{4}$ inches long) from inside of a spool of string for body.

Five lolly sticks for legs and neck.

One small cork for head.

Brown darning wool for mane.

Yellow felt and scraps of brown, black and white.

HOW TO MAKE HIM:

Cover the tube, cork and lolly sticks with yellow felt (figs. 1 and 4). Copying picture, sew these pieces together, being careful when attaching the legs to make sure they are level, so that the animal stands firmly. Cut out the pieces at the foot of this page; sew on tail and ears, stick on nose, eyes and pupils. Make the mane by sewing a row of brown woollen loops, cutting them through to make a fringe, or if you prefer, leave them intact. Cut small irregular shaped spots from brown felt and stick to body, upper part of legs and base of neck.

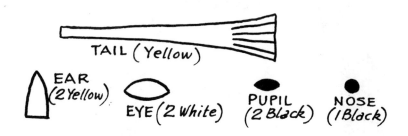

TAIL (Yellow)

EAR (2 Yellow)

EYE (2 White)

PUPIL (2 Black)

NOSE (1 Black)

Rupert the Rollicking Reindeer

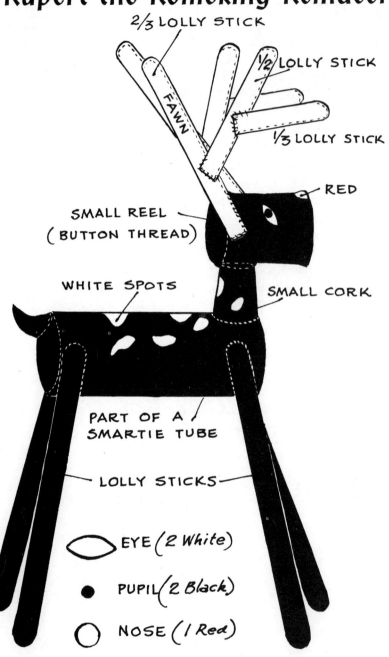

2/3 LOLLY STICK

FAWN

1/2 LOLLY STICK

1/3 LOLLY STICK

RED

SMALL REEL
(BUTTON THREAD)

WHITE SPOTS

SMALL CORK

PART OF A
SMARTIE TUBE

LOLLY STICKS

EYE (2 White)

PUPIL (2 Black)

NOSE (1 Red)

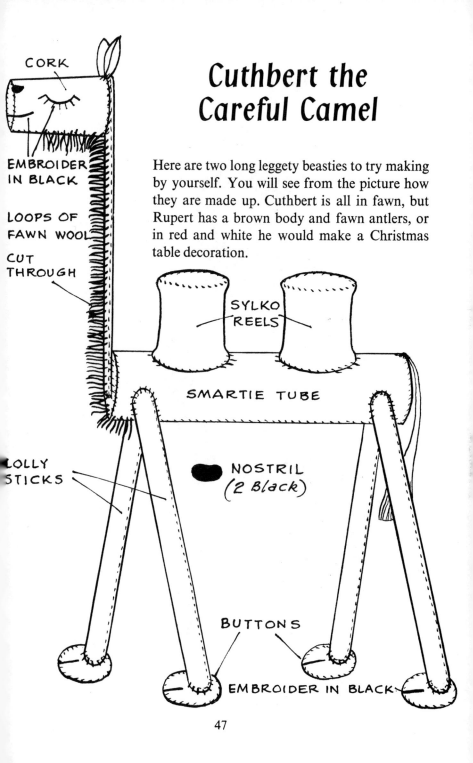

Cuthbert the Careful Camel

Here are two long leggety beasties to try making by yourself. You will see from the picture how they are made up. Cuthbert is all in fawn, but Rupert has a brown body and fawn antlers, or in red and white he would make a Christmas table decoration.

CORK

EMBROIDER IN BLACK

LOOPS OF FAWN WOOL

CUT THROUGH

SYLKO REELS

SMARTIE TUBE

LOLLY STICKS

NOSTRIL (2 Black)

BUTTONS

EMBROIDER IN BLACK

Willy the Wise Owl

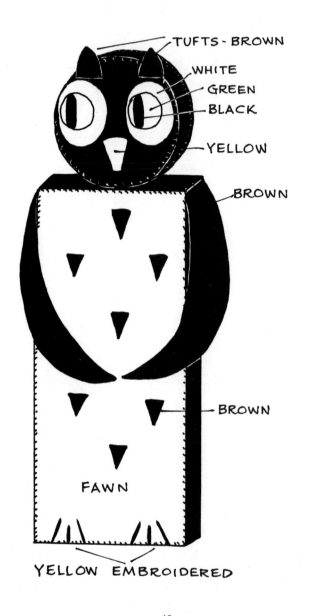

TUFTS - BROWN

WHITE

GREEN

BLACK

YELLOW

BROWN

BROWN

FAWN

YELLOW EMBROIDERED

YOU WILL NEED:

One rectangular box for body ($5\frac{1}{2} \times 1\frac{1}{4}$ inches).
One pill-box for head ($2\frac{1}{2}$ inches).
Brown felt and scraps of fawn, white, green, black and yellow.
Yellow stranded cotton.

HOW TO MAKE HIM:

Cover the pill-box with brown felt (fig. 1) and the larger box with brown on all sides except one (the front), for which use fawn. Cut out the pieces at the foot of this page. Stitch wings to shoulders and stick the tips to front of body as picture. Stick on eyes, beak, "tufts" and breast markings. Join head to body (fig. 2) and embroider feet in yellow stranded cotton.

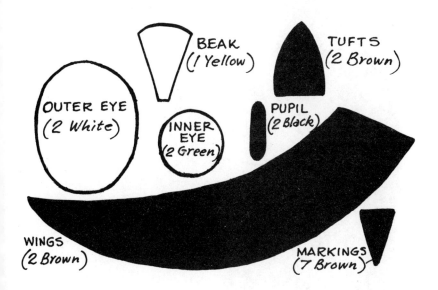

BEAK
(1 Yellow)

TUFTS
(2 Brown)

OUTER EYE
(2 White)

INNER EYE
(2 Green)

PUPIL
(2 Black)

WINGS
(2 Brown)

MARKINGS
(7 Brown)

Percy the Pill-box-head Penguin

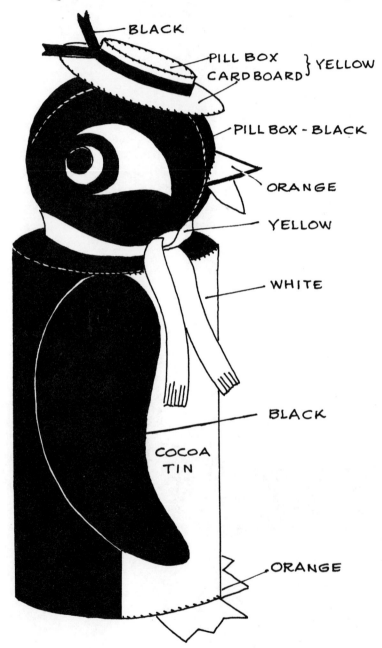

BLACK

PILL BOX
CARDBOARD } YELLOW

PILL BOX - BLACK

ORANGE

YELLOW

WHITE

BLACK

COCOA
TIN

ORANGE

YOU WILL NEED:

One cocoa-tin ($4\frac{1}{2}$ inches high) for body.
One pill-box ($2\frac{1}{2}$ inches) for head.
One pill-box ($1\frac{1}{2}$ inches) for hat.
One circle of stiff cardboard ($2\frac{3}{4}$ inches diameter).
Black, white, yellow and orange felt.

HOW TO MAKE HIM:

Cut out the pieces at the foot of this page. Cover the tin with black ends and back, and white front (fig. 1). This is the body; sew on the flippers and feet. Cover the large pill-box with black, and stick on the face markings. Sew head to body (fig. 2). Fold the beak in half and sew to head. Cover the cardboard circle and small pill-box in yellow, and sew these together for the hat, sew to head. Sew a strip of black felt $\frac{1}{4}$ inch wide $\times 7$ inches long all round the crown, leaving the ends loose at the back. Cut a strip of yellow felt 9 inches $\times \frac{1}{2}$ inch, fringe the ends and sew round the neck for a scarf.

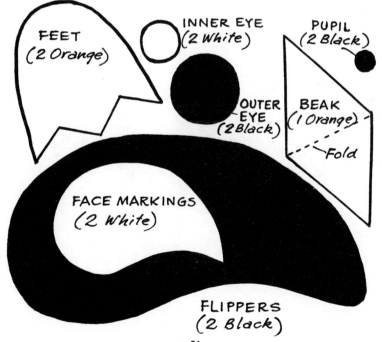

FEET
(2 Orange)

INNER EYE
(2 White)

PUPIL
(2 Black)

OUTER
EYE
(2 Black)

BEAK
(1 Orange)

Fold

FACE MARKINGS
(2 White)

FLIPPERS
(2 Black)

Clarence the Cotton-reel Chick

These little birds are simple to make from pill-boxes and cotton- or Sylko-reels. Sylko-reels (used for the chick) give a better shape. Cover these with a plain piece at the base (as fig. 1 for

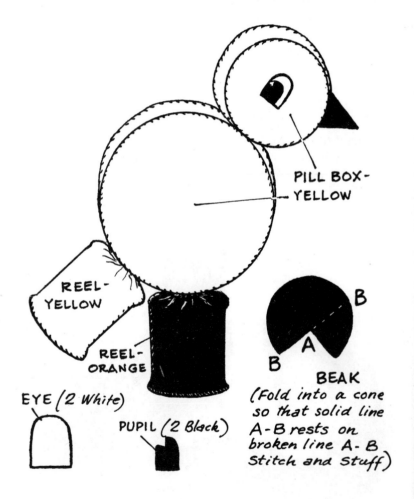

PILL BOX-
YELLOW

REEL-
YELLOW

REEL-
ORANGE

EYE (2 White)

PUPIL (2 Black)

B

A

B

BEAK
(Fold into a cone
so that solid line
A-B rests on
broken line A-B
Stitch and stuff)

Robin the Redbreast

the tins), but gather the top and draw it up (as fig. 8 for caterpillar). Sometimes it is difficult to make the birds balance, so experiment with the head and tail positions first, pinning them in place before sewing.

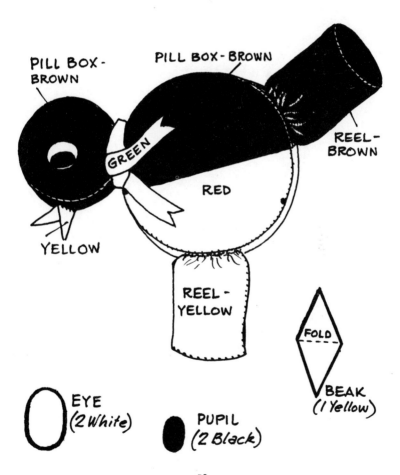

PILL BOX - BROWN

PILL BOX - BROWN

GREEN

REEL - BROWN

RED

YELLOW

REEL - YELLOW

FOLD

BEAK (1 Yellow)

EYE (2 White)

PUPIL (2 Black)

Miss Muffet's Spider

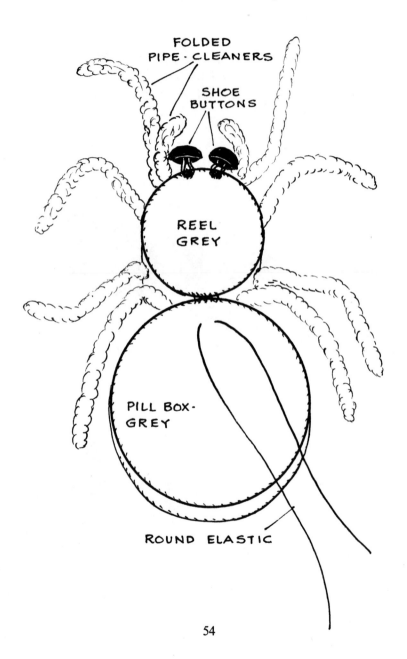

FOLDED
PIPE·CLEANERS

SHOE
BUTTONS

REEL
GREY

PILL BOX·
GREY

ROUND ELASTIC

YOU WILL NEED:

One pill-box (2 inches) for body.
One empty reel Sylko size for head.
Two black shoe-buttons for eyes.
Eighteen pipe-cleaners.
Grey felt.
Length of round elastic.

HOW TO MAKE HIM:

Twist the pipe-cleaners together in pairs and then double together again (fig. 9, *A* and *B*, page 58). Bend one of these to a hairpin shape (fig. 9, *C*) and using adhesive tape stick on top of reel (fig. 5, *A*) for the "palps". Turn reel upside down and stick the remaining eight twisted pipe-cleaners in place for legs (fig. 5, *B*). Cover the box and reel with grey felt (fig. 5, *C*), leaving the legs and "palps" protruding and sewing firmly between these. Join reel (head) and box (body) as picture. Sew on two black shoe-buttons for eyes and bend the legs upwards and then downwards into "arches". Thread a piece of round elastic through the back, from which to dangle the spider.

Fig. 5. Making Spider's head.

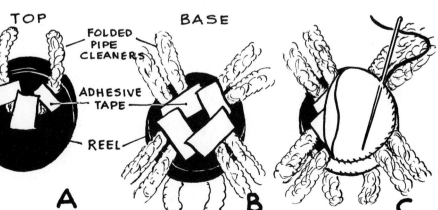

Clarissa the

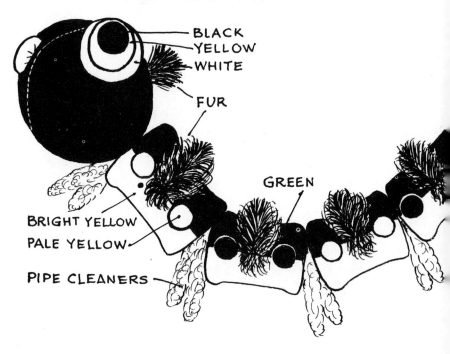

BLACK
YELLOW
WHITE

FUR

GREEN

BRIGHT YELLOW
PALE YELLOW

PIPE CLEANERS

YOU WILL NEED:

One pill-box ($2\frac{1}{2}$ inches diameter) for head.

Nine empty reels (Sylko size) for body.

Three large buttons ($1\frac{1}{4}$ inches diameter) for eyes and sucker.

One smaller button ($\frac{3}{4}$ inch diameter) for nose.

Eighteen pipe-cleaners for legs.

Scraps of fur.

Green, black, white, pale and bright yellow felt.

About 18 inches wire (galvanised, gauge 14).

HOW TO MAKE HER:

Lay the wire round the edge of the box for 2 inches and stick in place with adhesive tape, covering the sharp point (fig. 6). Cover box with green felt, making a hole in the strip which goes round

56

Cotton-reel Caterpillar

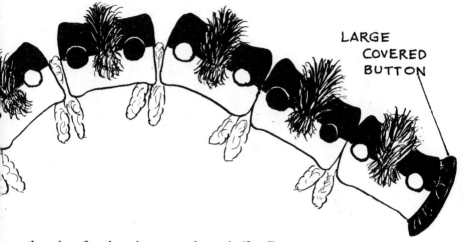

LARGE
COVERED
BUTTON

the edge, for the wire to go through (fig. 7).

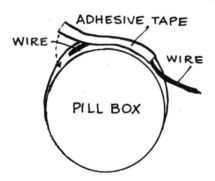

Fig. 6. Covering sharp end of wire.

Fig. 7. Covering box
with wire protruding.

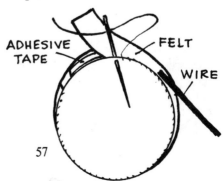

Cover eight of the reels, so that one side is green and one bright yellow (fig. 8).

Fig. 8. Covering reels—gathering method.

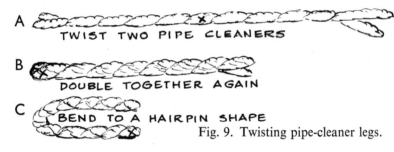

Fig. 9. Twisting pipe-cleaner legs.

Twist the pipe-cleaners together in pairs and double together again, so that there are four thicknesses; bend to a hairpin shape (fig. 9). These are the legs. Sew one of these to each covered reel (fig. 10). Sew a narrow strip of fur round the centre

Fig. 10. Attaching legs to reel.

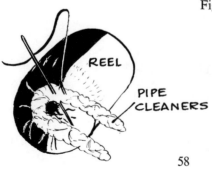

of the green half of each reel and thread the reels on to the wire, legs to the front. Cover the ninth reel (which could be a long slim one, such as Lurex thread), lower half only, leaving the top half open for the present (fig. 11, *A*). Sew on the pipe-cleaner legs. Thread this on to wire, completed half first (fig. 11, *B*).

Fig. 11. Finishing off tail end of Caterpillar.

Pushing the reels as tightly together as possible, and using pliers, bend the end of the wire down over the reel and bind with adhesive tape to cover the sharp ends (fig. 11, *C*). Finish sewing up the side seam on this reel and gather up and finish off the end. Cover the small button with pale yellow felt, two of the large ones with white and one with green (fig. 12). Sew the yellow one in place for a nose, the green at the tip of the tail for a "sucker" and the white ones for eyes, gathers inwards and smooth side showing. Following the picture, stick on the eye markings and spots, also a tuft of fur on the head. You can, of course, use as many or as few reels as you like for Clarissa, and she will bend to any shape.

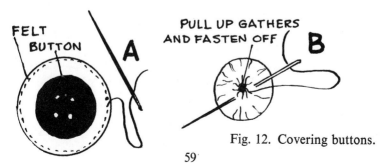

Fig. 12. Covering buttons.

59

Ideas for using your Toys

1. Fill some of the tins used for the Roly-Poly Rascals with a few beads, pebbles or peas and use them as babies' rattles. (For ideas for flower, flag and animal head rattles see *Modern Soft Toy Making*, Section IV.)

2. Make several Tubular Tommies to use as skittles.

3. Make animals to go with the Noah Family, in a procession of "two's", taking your ideas from the Long Leggety Beasties. Older children in a school could make these for the kindergarten department.

4. Illustrate some nursery rhymes. Tube-tin Topsy could be enlarged to become Miss Muffet—her spider is on page 54.

5. Try making a zoo. The cages could be made from lolly sticks.

6. Bring in the whole family to make a Nativity Scene at Christmas-time. The Shepherds and Kings could easily be based on the shape of Simpering Cynthia. Use the Camel on page 47. and invent an Ox and Ass.

7. Make small toys in gay Christmassy colours to use as decorations for the tree, adding a little sparkle in the form of sequins. Turn some of the little figures into Father Christmas or a Snowman and if you want them to sit on top of a branch, sew a pipe cleaner to the base and twist this tightly to the tree.

8. Teenagers, make a collection of amusing creatures for your bedroom.

9. Try making the dachshund on the Contents page—his head is the tin from a puncture repair outfit and his neck a cotton-reel. He was designed and made by a ten-year-old boy.